Balloon Lagoon

and the magic islands of poetry

by
Adrian Mitchell

illustrated by Tony Ross

ORCHARD BOOKS

**to my wife Celia
to my children and grand-children
to my nieces and nephews and their children
to my parents
to my animals
to all the children and teachers who have made poetry with me**

to the writers who delighted me most when I was a child:
Hans Christian Andersen, Anon, F. Anstey, M. E. Atkinson,
R. M. Ballantyne, Helen Bannerman, J. M. Barrie, R. D. Blackmore,
William Blake, Robert Browning, Jean de Brunhoff, John Buchan,
John Bunyan, Edgar Rice Burroughs, Lewis Carroll, G. K. Chesterton,
Leslie Charteris, Richmal Crompton, Daniel Defoe, Walter de la Mare,
Charles Dickens, Arthur Conan Doyle, Wanda Gag, H. L. Gee, Kenneth
Grahame, the Brothers Grimm, Gunby Hadath, H. Rider Haggard,
Richard Jefferies, Captain W. E. Johns, Erich Kästner, John Keats,
Rudyard Kipling, Andrew Lang, Stephen Leacock, Edward Lear,
Hugh Lofting, André Maurois, Arthur Mee, A. A. Milne, Edith Nesbit,
George Orwell, Beatrix Potter, Arthur Ransome, Dean Swift,
Robert Louis Stevenson, Alfred Lord Tennyson, Katharine Tozer,
Mark Twain, Jules Verne, H. G. Wells, Percy F. Westerman, T. H. White,
Walt Whitman, P. G. Wodehouse and Johann D. Wyss as well as the
makers of *Chick's Own, The Dandy, The Beano, The Rover,
The Wag's Handbook, The Boy's Own Paper, Punch, Batman,
Superman* and *Green Lantern*

to all those who work as writers, illustrators, publishers, booksellers,
librarians and parents, to bring children exciting and beautiful books

to you

Adrian Mitchell

Acknowledgements

Many of these poems have never been published before, but others appeared in *Nothingmas Day* (Allison and Busby) and *All My Own Stuff* (Simon and Schuster Young Books) which are both out of print, also in *Adrian Mitchell's Greatest Hits* (Bloodaxe Books), *Blue Coffee* (Bloodaxe) and *The Orchard Book of Poems* (Orchard Books).

EDUCATIONAL HEALTH WARNING

None of these poems or any other work by Adrian Mitchell is to be used in connection with any examination or test whatsoever. But I'm glad if people who like them read them aloud, sing them, dance them or act them in schools. And even happier if they choose to learn any of them by heart.

Magic Islands

Whenever I feel super-brave
I ghost away from my PC
To follow the secret, sandy path
Leading down to the shores of the Daydream Sea.

And I sail away in my Skylark boat
While our blue-green sail is followed by birds
And I drop my wide net down through the waves
In the hope of catching some fishy words.

But if I haul some word-fishes aboard
I pick the best ones out of the heap
And draw their portraits lovingly –
Then throw them all back into the deep.

Sail on, sail on, my little boat,
Round this shining archipelago.
Look down – the underwater city
Of great Atlantis, far below.

Sail on, sail on, the mermaids sing,
A lighthouse sword cuts through the dark.
The fountain of the Great White Whale!
The Woofmiaou Isles where purr meets bark!

We'll ride the whirlpools and the storms,
We'll dodge Iceberg Academy too
And fight the Giant Octopus
And Captain Bloodshot's desperate Crew.

Balloon Lagoon, Elephantasia,
Spookalulu where the zombies crawl.
Mysteriosa and The Rampages –
My boat and I visit them all.

The Skylark's eager to be off,
So hop on board and sail with me
Together we'll explore today
The Magic Islands of Poetry.

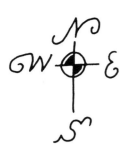

Contents

Mysteriosa

The Rampages

The Woofmiaou Isles

Iceberg Academy

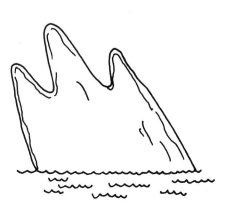

Contents

Elephantasia

Spookalulu

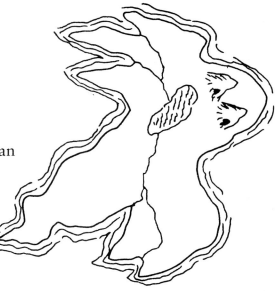

Balloon Lagoon

Mysteriosa

secret land of magic, mind-mazes and marmalade

The Woman of Water

There once was a woman of water
Refused a Wizard her hand.
So he took the tears of a statue
And the weight from a grain of sand
And he squeezed the sap from a comet
And the height from a cypress tree
And he drained the dark from midnight
And he charmed the brains from a bee
And he soured the mixture with thunder
And stirred it with ice from hell
And the woman of water drank it down
And she changed into a well.

There once was a woman of water
Who was changed into a well
And the well smiled up at the Wizard
And down down down that old Wizard fell...

Stufferation

Lovers lie around in it
Broken glass is found in it
Grass
I like that stuff

Tuna fish get trapped in it
Legs come wrapped in it
Nylon
I like that stuff

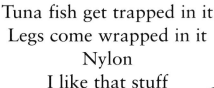

Eskimos and tramps chew it
Madame Tussaud gave status to it
Wax
I like that stuff

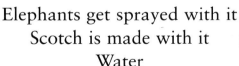

Elephants get sprayed with it
Scotch is made with it
Water
I like that stuff

Clergy are dumbfounded by it
Bones are surrounded by it
Flesh
I like that stuff

Harps are strung with it
Mattresses are sprung with it
Wire
I like that stuff

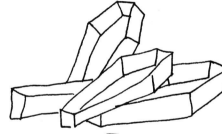

Carpenters make cots of it
Undertakers use lots of it
Wood
I like that stuff

Dirty cigarettes are lit by it
Pensioners get happy when they sit by it
Fire
I like that stuff

Johnny Dankworth's alto is made of it, most of it*
Scoobdidoo is composed of it**
Plastic
I like that stuff

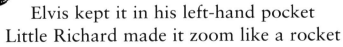

Elvis kept it in his left-hand pocket
Little Richard made it zoom like a rocket
Rock 'n' Roll
Ooh my soul
I like that stuff

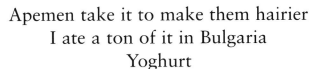

Apemen take it to make them hairier
I ate a ton of it in Bulgaria
Yoghurt
I like that stuff

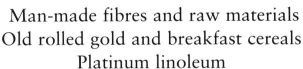

Man-made fibres and raw materials
Old rolled gold and breakfast cereals
Platinum linoleum
I like that stuff

Skin on my hands
Hair on my head
Toenails on my feet
And linen on the bed

Well I like that stuff
Yes I like that stuff
The earth
Is made of earth
And I like that stuff

*Jazz musician John Dankworth used to play a plastic saxophone.

**Scoobdidoo was a fistful of kind of multi-coloured pieces of plastic which were a playground craze in the 1950s. It was a sad sort of toy, nothing like the exciting Hula Hoop of the same period.

Mesopotamia

I dreamed I was sailing on dusty waters
Mesopotamia Mesopotamia
There were two yellow rivers merged into one river
Mesopotamia Mesopotamia
My boat had a woven cabin for shade
And a golden double sail like an eagle in flight
And a woman who sang to me like marmalade
As we sailed in the direction of the night

Nothingmas Day

No it wasn't.

It was Nothingmas Eve and all the children in Notown were not
tingling with excitement as they lay unawake in their heaps.
D
   o
      w
        n
           s
              t
                  a
                     r

                s their parents were busily not placing
the last crackermugs, glimmerslips and sweetlumps on the
Nothingmas Tree.

Hey! But what was that invisible trail of chummy sparks
or vaulting stars across the sky?
    Father Nothingmas – drawn by 18 or 21 rainmaidens!
    Father Nothingmas – his sackbut bulging with air!
    Father Nothingmas – was not on his way!
(From the streets of the snowless town came the quiet of unsung
carols and the merry silence of the steeple bell.)

Next morning the children did not fountain out of bed with cries
of WHOOPERATION! They picked up their Nothingmas
Stockings and with traditional quiperamas such as: "Look what
I haven't got! It's just what I didn't want!" pulled their stockings
on their ordinary legs.

For breakfast they ate – breakfast.

After woods they all avoided the Nothingmas Tree, where Daddy, his face failing to beam like a leaky torch, was not distributing gemgames, sodaguns, golly-trolleys, jars of humdrums and packets of slubberated croakers.

Off, off, off went the children to school, soaking each other with no howls of "Merry Nothingmas and a Happy No Year!", and not pulping each other with no-balls.

At school Miss Whatnot taught them how to write No Thank You Letters.

Home they burrowed for Nothingmas Dinner.
The table was not groaning under all manner of

    NO TURKEY
    NO SPICED HAM
    NO SPROUTS
    NO CRANBERRY JELLYSAUCE
    NO NOT NOWT
There was not one (1) shoot of glee as the Nothingmas Pudding, unlit, was not brought in. Mince pies were not available, nor was there any demand for them.

Then, as another Nothingmas clobbered to a close, they all haggled off to bed where they slept happily never after.

    and that is not the end of the story...

My Last Nature Walk

I strode among the clumihacken
Where scrubble nudges to the barfter
Till I whumped into, hidden in the bracken,
A groolted after-laughter-rafter.

(For milty Wah-Zohs do guffaw
Upon a laughter-rafter perch.
But after laughter they balore
Unto a second beam to gurch.)
Yet here was but one gollamonce!
I glumped upon the after-laughter-rafter.
Where was its other-brother? Oh! My bonce!
The Wah-Zohs blammed it with a laughter-rafter.

Moral: Never gamble on a bramble ramble.

Glossary:
clumihacken – the old stalks of wild Brussels sprouts
scrubble – unusually tall moss, often scuffed
the barfter – the height at which low clouds cruise
to whump – to bump into, winding oneself in the process
groolted – cunningly engraved with the portraits of
    little-known and famous barbers
milty – clean but mean-minded
Wah-Zohs – French birds, sometimes spelt Oiseaux
to balore – to hover fatly downwards
to gurch – to recover from cheerfulness
gollamonce – a thing that is sought for desperately,
    although there is no good reason for finding it
to glump – to glump
to blam – to shonk on the cloddle

The Village Pond Has Good Words For Everybody

to the grass it says	green
to the swan it says	whitest
to the breeze	ripples
to the heron	welcome
to the summer	coolness
to the winter	ice
to the fishes	green whitest
	ripples welcome
	coolness ice home

Construction Kit Paint Invention

Dip the brush provided in your can
Of Detacho-Paint.
Detacho-Paint the surface
Of the limb or digit or organ required.
Allow half an hour
For the subtle molecular change
Brought about by Detacho-Paint.
Now you can painlessly remove, by hand,
That limb, digit or organ.

You can take off your fingers one by one
And plant them in your armpits.
You can take off your nose
And stick it to the back of your neck.
You can take off your arms and legs
And swap them with your friends.
They still work fine.
They've still got feelings.
Switch your ears for your feet with Detacho-Paint.
Take off your head and have a good game
Of volley-ball with your bonce.

I remember Meccano
With its flat little spanners
And fiddly nuts and bolts
And scraping the paint of red and blue girders
And the sadness of Meccano animals,
So skeletal, so full of holes,
So unlike anything except Meccano.

And I remember my Bayko Building Set,
With its silver rods rising hopefully
From a green bakelite base,
Waiting for red bricks, white bricks and green bricks
To be slid down into place between them
Eventually forming a rather forbidding model
Of a suburban public convenience.

I even remember Minibrix,
Those ceramic bricks the size of fingernails,
The colour of baked beans,
Which had to be stuck into place with toy cement
And soaked apart again, but that took months...

I even remember a primitive kind of Lego
Made of smelly red rubber
And also other, sillier construction kits
Involving warped wooden rods, elastic bands
And clockwork motors.
All of them came in boxes
Picturing boys in shorts with polished hair
Dwarfed by models of steam engines and Eiffel Towers.
All of them defeated me utterly, utterly.

But now I have my happy Revenge
For I can become a construction kit myself.
I simply dip the brush into Detacho-Paint
And paint the surface
Of my body, my limbs, my head
And proceed, gradually, with great pleasure
To take myself to pieces.

And then I put myself together again
To form an entirely different model.

Maya's Song

Face after face after face after face –
The city is a most faceful place.
So I run to the countryside scenery
And chameleon into its greenery.
O the faces of cities both jagged and kind
Go gently slipping out of my mind
And the only face I can see pretty soon
Is the so-what face of the snowy moon.

Watch Your Step – I'm Drenched

In Manchester there are a thousand puddles.
Bus-queue puddles poised on slanting paving stones,
Railway puddles slouching outside stations,
Cinema puddles in ambush at the exits,
Zebra-crossing puddles in dips of the dark stripes –
They lurk in the murk
Of the north-western evening
For the sake of their notorious joke,
Their only joke – to soak
The tights or trousers of the citizens.
Each splash and consequent curse is echoed by
One thousand dark Mancunian puddle chuckles.

In Manchester there lives the King of Puddles,
Master of Miniature Muck Lakes,
The Shah of Slosh, Splendifero of Splash,
Prince, Pasha and Pope of Puddledom.
Where? Somewhere. The rain-headed ruler
Lies doggo, incognito,
Disguised as an average, accidental mini-pool.
He is as scared as any other emperor,
For one night, all his soiled and soggy victims
Might storm his streets, assassination in their minds,
A thousand rolls of blotting paper in their hands,
And drink his shadowed, one-joke life away.

Patchwork Rap

I'm a touch lazy
Don't like doing much work
But often get the itch
To pitch into some patchwork
It may be a hotchpotch
Like fretwork or such work
When I slouch on my couch
And I fetch out my patchwork

First I snatch a patch
From the batch in my pouch
But the patch doesn't match
The patches on my patchwork
So I catch another patch
From the batch in my satchel
And this one matches
The patches on my patchwork
So I take my patch
Attach it with stitches
Patch against patch
Where the patchwork matches
But if it doesn't match
Even after it's attached
Then the mismatched stitch
Has to be detached...

You know
I don't like thatchwork
Don't like ditchwork
Only kind I favour
Is my patchwork stitchwork

And soon my patchwork's
Going like clockwork
Sharper than a pitchfork
Neater than brickwork
Hotter than a firework
Cooler than a waxwork

So I snatch a patch
From the batch in my pouch
But the patch doesn't match
The patches on my patchwork
So I catch another patch
From the batch in my satchel
And this one matches
The patches on my patchwork
So I take my patch
Attach it with stitches
Patch against patch
Where the patchwork matches
And I keep on patching
Till everything's matching
And I keep on stitching
Till I've filled up the kitchen
With my rich rich rich rich
Wider than a soccer pitch
Wonderful colourful magical patchwork quilt!

Now which stitch is which?

A Sticky End

Jar of marmalade
Marmalade jar
What a beautiful
Shining person you are
For the marmalade germs
Are mortified
To see those dark
Orangey chunks inside
Which recline in the depths
Of a succulent glade
In a miniature jungle
Of marmalade

Like a castle of crystal
Your glass wall resists
The beating of microbes'
Puny fists
And a million bacteria
Cannot remove
Your golden-rimmed lid
From its stickysweet groove

Jar of marmalade
Marmalade jar
What a beautiful
Shining person you are
You defy the decay
Of the world at large
To save all your treasures
For my bread and marge

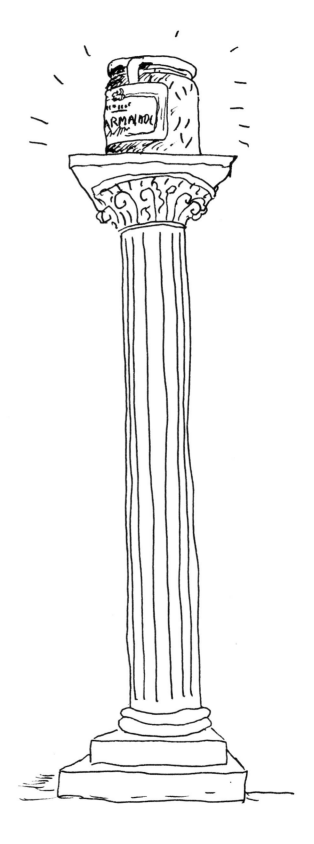

Jar of marmalade
Jar of might
I lifted you up
The other night
For I fancied a just-after-midnight snack
But alas! the last eater
Who put you back
Had only replaced
And not screwed down the lid
By which I raised you
And so in mid-
Air you sadly
Detached yourself
And bounced askance
From a lower-down shelf
And crashed to a splintery, splungey doom
On the cruel tiles
Of the gobsmacked room

Jar as bright
As the Land of Oz
What a beautiful
Shining person you was

Yes

A smile says: Yes.
A heart says: Blood.
When the rain says: Drink,
The earth says: Mud.

The kangaroo says: Trampoline.
Giraffes say: Tree.
A bus says: Us,
While a car says: Me.

Lemon trees say: Lemons.
A jug says: Lemonade.
The villain says: You're wonderful.
The hero: I'm afraid.

The forest says: Hide and Seek.
The grass says: Green and Grow.
The railway says: Maybe.
The prison says: No.

The millionaire says: Take.
The beggar says: Give.
The soldier cries: Mother!
The baby sings: Live.

The river says: Come with me.
The moon says: Bless.
The stars say: Enjoy the light.
The sun says: Yes.

The Rampages

amongst whose ragged rocks run riot
some of the toughest, daftest and most amazing
kids still at large

Dumb Insolence

I'm big for ten years old
Maybe that's why they get at me

Teachers, parents, cops
Always getting at me

When they get at me

I don't hit em
They can do you for that

I don't swear at em
They can do you for that

I stick my hands in my pockets
And stare at them

And while I stare at them
I think about sick

They call it dumb insolence

They don't like it
But they can't do you for it

Ode To Dennis The Menace And His Gang

There are Four Seasons of the Beano:

Chocolate Eggs!
    Sandcastle Contest!
        Fireworks!
and

    Xmas Stocking!

Oh Xmas Stocking! Favourite Season!
When all along the top of the fat word

    BEANO

lies
like a generous layer of icing on the cakes in a box of tuck

    Snow! As in Snowmen!
    Snow! As in Snowballs!

    Snow!
Snow!   Snow!   Snow!
    which falls and drifts in every Reader's dreams

Techno-Child

My dad was a kung fu fighter in a video game called
    Death Cult Army
He lurked around on the seventh level waiting for smug
    contestants so he could chop them up like salami
He was good for nothing but kick jab punch gouge headbutt
    kick in the bum
And all his friends were stuperollificated when he fell in love
    and married my mum

My mum was a thirty-two colour hologram at a Medical
    Convention in Beverly Hills
She represented the Statue of Liberty and she advertised
    Anti-Indigestion Pills
She was half the size of the statue itself and the tourists
    she attracted were fewer
And if you ever reached out to touch her robes, well
    your hand just went straight through her

They met in the Robocop Theme Park on a hullabaloo
    of a night
When my dad saw off some Gremlins on Camels who
    had challenged mum to a fight
They sat together and watched the moon from a
    swing-chair on Popeye's porch
Then my father proposed in Japanese and my mother
    she dropped her torch

They were married and put on a floppy disc by
    the Bishop of IBM
Pac-Man, Count Duckula and all the Power Rangers
    came and celebrated with them
The fun was going ballistic but it nearly ended
    in tears
For those old Space Invaders started a ruck with
    the Mortal Kombateers

Since my mum's a mirage of electrons and my dad
    is strictly 2-D
You may wonder how I was born at all in this
    Virtual Reality
Well they're close as a Mouse and its Mouse-mat
    and they taught me just what I should do –
I fight video-gamesters and indigestion with
    pills and a torch and kung fu.

Bebe Belinda And Carl Columbus

verses for Laura

There was a girl who threw bananas about
When she couldn't get bananas she threw baseball bats about
When she couldn't get baseball bats she threw big blue
    beehives about
And her name was Bebe, Bebe Belinda

There was a boy who threw cuckoo clocks about
When he couldn't find cuckoo clocks he threw cucumbers about
When he couldn't find cucumbers he went crackers and threw
    christening cakes about
And his name was Carl, Carl Columbus

In Hanover Terrace, that magical place,
Bebe and Carl met, face to red face.
She bust his cuckoo clock with a bunch of bananas.
In a swashbuckling sword fight his cucumber cutlass
Carved her baseball bat to bits.
She bashed him on the bonce with her best blue beehive
But he craftily crowned her with a christening cake.

And they left it to me, old Lizzie Lush
To clean up the street with my scrubbing brush.

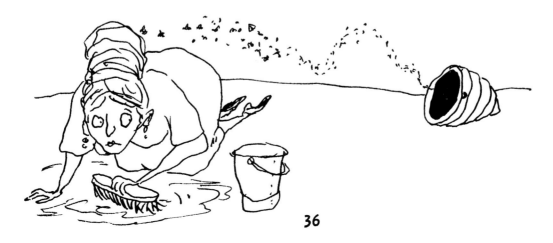

36

Watching You Skating

I see two skates
Blue sliding into silver
Silver gliding into blue

I see two moons
One moon reflected in each of the skates
Carrying you

You zip across the blue and silver pond
I am wonderfully fond
Of the moon and the moon-faced pond and you

One Bad Word

*(To my Black friends and their children and others
who are sometimes taunted with ugly names by fools.)*

You call me that bad word
That one bad word
That bad word weighs a thousand tonne
That one bad word burns my skin all over
You call me one bad word
That word makes my mother
Cast down her eyes in shame
Makes my father
Deny his own name
Makes my brother
Turn and fight like a demon
Makes my sister
Spend her life in bad dreaming

So call me one bad word
And you don't know what will happen
It could be tears it could be blood
It could be storm
It could be silence
It could be a rage
Hot enough to burn the whole town down
Could be a stampede of elephants
Through your back garden
And into your mother's
Frilly perfume sitting room
Could be zombie nightmares
Every night for the rest
Of your natural life
Could be all your food

From this day on
Will taste of rotten fishheads
Could be anything
Could be the end of the world
But mostly likely
This will follow:

I'll stare at you
For one cold second
And then I'll turn and walk away from you
Leaving you alone with yourself
And your one bad word

Beattie's Beliefs

God made the world
God made ballet
God made everything

except fireworks

Nobody From Nowhere

The Nurse she said:
What you doing in bed?
I said: nothing.
The Matron came
And asked: What's your name?
I said: nobody.
The Student with his comb
Said: Where's your home?
I said: nowhere.
The Doctor prodded,
The Doctor nodded.
I heard the Doctor say:
Who are you anyway?
I said: nobody.

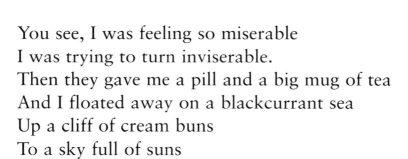

You see, I was feeling so miserable
I was trying to turn inviserable.
Then they gave me a pill and a big mug of tea
And I floated away on a blackcurrant sea
Up a cliff of cream buns
To a sky full of suns

And I don't know how it happened
But I know I was rapping
Yes flying over London
With my pyjamas flapping

I was munching marshmallows
In the marshes of Mars
And I whooshed through the Milky Way's
Sherbet of stars

Then I was hopping on the Moon
With my galactic Mum
Till I tripped on some Krypton
And landed on my bum.

And my eyes began to open
And I heard the Nurse say:
You've had your operation –
How are you today?
Nobody from Nowhere,
Do you feel OK?

I'm not Nobody
From Nowhere, mate,
I'm the Famous Somebody
And I feel great
And I just had a brilliant
Operation Dream
And so, by golly,
Wheel me in a trolley
Full of Planetary Pizza
Space Jelly and Moony Ice Cream.

Westminster Children's Hospital

Poem For Amy

Poetry can be a lonely walk
Down a dark forest pathway
Without an end.
So it lifts the heart to see the brightness
Of a welcoming new friend.

What's that wonderful, warmful light
Shining out a thousand miles?
All the animals of the world start dancing –
When Amy smiles.

A Game To Play With Babies

Ring the bell – ding ding
Press the buzzer – bzzzzzz
Knock at the door – knock knock
And walk in – oh, no thank you!

(The way to play. Ring the bell – pull the earlobe.
Press the buzzer – press the tip of the nose.
Knock at the door – tap the forehead.
And walk in – put your little finger in mouth and withdraw
*   it quickly before you're bitten saying, "Oh, no thank you!"*
It's best to demonstrate all these movements and words
on yourself a few times until the baby has got the idea.
Then you try the baby's earlobe, nose, forehead and mouth,
but very gently. Be careful with the fourth move – some
babies have tiger teeth. You will find that most babies
enjoy this game, especially after the twentieth repetition.)

Ode To My Nose

O Nose
Why perch upon my Face?
Could you not find
A better place?

You jut between
One Eye and tother
So neither Eye
Can see his Brother.

An easy target
For the hostile Fist.
You're an obstruction
When I want to be kissed.

And when you run
It's always South
Over my top lip
Into my Mouth.

O Nose
Why perch upon my Face?
Could you discover
No better place?

My Nose replied:
Up here I have come
As far as possible
From your Bum.

The Battle-Hymn Of The Ice-Cream Connoisseur

Mine eyes have seen the glory of Pink Fudge Sundaes
I guzzle 'em on Saturdays and slurp on Mondays
I smuggle 'em to chapel in my Grandma's undies
As my stomach rumbles on.

Awful Medical Poem

If I had a rusty concrete mixer
I would fill it with Murcheson's Cough Elixir.
Doesn't the thought of it make you sick, sir?

Fruit Jokes

The satsuma
Has no sense of
humour
But a fig'll
Giggle

My Yellow Jumper

When I ride a banana
At the local gymkhana
I usually win
By a skin

Deep Sherbet

deep sherbet
in a cardboard
cylinder
printed red
and yellow

used to poke
my liquorice
tube down through
the top and sucked

and when the sherbet
hit the spittle
on my palate –
that's when the fizz began

The Woofmiaou Isles

home of noble-minded dogs
and conniving cats

In The Country With Billie

With both hands I lift her
High over my hat
And she growls as I call her
My Flying Cat,

Then down to my shoulder
And round my back
She curls like a scarf
Of white and black.

As I climb through the woods
In my purring scarf
Why do the squirrels
And hedgehogs laugh?

She keeps me warm
When the rain blows chilly –
My black-coated, white-booted
Friend called Billie.

Singapore Sausage Cat

Behold the cat
the cat full of sausage
his ears do slope backwards
his coat's full of glossage

His whiskers extend
like happy antennae
he would count his blessings
but they are too many

He unfoldeth his limbs
he displayeth his fur
he narrows his eyes
and begins to purr

And his purring is smooth
as an old tree's mossage –
Behold the cat
who is full of sausage

I Walk Two Dogs

(for Ella and Judy)

I walk two dogs.
On her black lead and chain
Trots my Marilyn Monroe retriever
With all her golden feathers flowing.

I walk two dogs.
On her small red lead
Runs an old Jack Russell like a country aunt.
Just above her tail she wears a large black blot
Which indicates where she likes to be patted.

I walk two dogs,
Their paths are intertwined.
When we reach Hampstead Heath and their freedom
They glance around, making up their minds
Where we're supposed to go.

Monroe's an archaeologist,
Her aunt is an explorer,
So the retriever digs
While the Jack Russell gets as lost as she can.
I go for walks in two directions at once,
Though sometimes they graze on the scents in the grass,
Muzzles together in the smoky early morning.

I call them to me, I fix their leads.
As I follow them home I feel like the sail
Of a ship of gold and black and white.
I walk two dogs
I walk two dogs
I walk them on two leads
Held in one hand.

Footnote To 'I Walk Two Dogs'

I boastfully wrote 'I Walk Two Dogs'
Then went to catch a bus and passed a fellow
Walking six greyhounds on their leads
Dressed in long coats of black and yellow.
They were strong and perfectly-formed and clean
Like the components of a submarine.

For Golden Ella

At four in the morning
With furry tread
My good dog climbs
Aboard my bed

She lays her chin
In my open palm
Now neither of us
Can come to harm

In my open hand
Her long jaw seems
Like a shifting weight
As she chews at her dreams

From the coolness
Of her nose
The blessing of
Her breathing glows

And the bad night
Vampires disappear
As my wrist is tickled
By her ear

To My Dog

This gentle beast
This golden beast
laid her long chin
along my wrist

and my wrist
is branded
with her love
and trust

and the salt of my cheek
is hers to lick
so long as I
or she shall last

A Poem For Dogs

(I know plenty of poems about dogs but this is the only one I ever wrote for a dog, a golden retriever called Polly. She liked to listen to it while her chest was being tickled. Try it on a dog you love, changing the name of course, and reciting it over and over in a gentle, deep voice. You will find that most dogs enjoy this game, especially after supper.)

Good Polly
Good dog.
Good Polly,
Good dog.

For Number Ten

One out of ten, six gold, four black.
Born in a bulging, transparent sack.

I eased him out, this holy gift.
His mother turned to him and sniffed

Then licked the blood and the sack away.
All small and golden, there he lay.

There are some insects and some flowers
Whose life is spent in twenty-four hours.

For twenty-four hours, beside his mother,
He fed and he slept with his sisters and brothers.

Good smells. Close warm. Then a crushing weight.
Then nothing at all. His head the wrong shape.

He was wrapped up and taken beyond the bounds
Of his mother's familiar digging grounds

For she would have found him and known him too
And have wept as golden retrievers do.

So she kept all her love for the alive –
The black four and the golden five.

But I celebrate that golden pup
Whom I talked to and kissed as I wrapped him up.

For he fed and he slept and was loved as he lay
In the dark where he spent one golden day.

Now his mother pursues an eccentric trail
With casual sweeps of her lavish gold tail

And when number ten stumbles into my mind
She consoles me and so do the other nine.

Epitaph For A Golden Retriever

It was my job
To be a dog

My master said
That I was good

Now I turn myself around
And lie down in the musky ground

A Cat Called Slumber

In the middle of the night appears
My day-shy tabby with collapsible ears
And I stroke her head so those ears collapse
And she purrs to say that she loves me, perhaps

My Cat Slumber Speaks Of Celia

At five in the morning when my human is asleep
I stalk on to her eiderdown and crouch on her
Oh she's a warm and friendly-smelling heap
So I purr and I purr and I purr

Iceberg Academy

the only floating shipwrecked school in the known universe

Five Years Old

Five-year-olds dream of becoming giants –
Golden-bearded, striding around the map,
Gulping streams, munching sandwiches
Of crushed ice and white-hot anthracite
Between two slices of slate.
They sit on the edge of Salisbury Plain
Bawling huge songs across the counties
For ten days at a time,
Eating trees, cuddling carthorses,
Before stomping home to Windsor Castle.
They name clouds. They fall in love with buses,
They lick the stars, they are amazed by hoses,
They dance all the time because they don't think about dancing...

They long to be allowed into the big good schools
Which will teach them to be giants with wings.

Amazing Mathematical Discovery Rocks Universe. Essex Man Slightly Hurt.

Nobel Maths Wizards Make Odd Discovery –
Two Plus Two Has Stopped Making Four.

TWO PLUS TWO MAKES FIVE AND A BIT!

Schoolkids Burn Dummies of Einstein and Newton,
Those old dummies, as they chant:
Two Plus Two Makes Five And A Bit!

Their faulty arithmetic finally exposed –
Suspension bridges go haywire!
Skyscrapers sway, fold and collapse into their own cellars!
Cash registers, calculators and computers
Short-circuit themselves in mass suicide.
The Thames fills up with stockbrokers and Vatmen!

Only the average people
Whose maths is so far below average
Go about their normal unbusinesslike business –
Making things without measuring them exactly,
Only pretending to count the change,
Buying Two and Two
And being charged Five And A Bit.

The Secret Number Burrow

Only its whiskers showed above the ground.
Its squat head and odd-sided body were covered
By the deep dust. I reached down and found
The scruff of its skull, pulled it up. I'd discovered
The number which hides between Eight and Nine.
It is called *Shtoogeree*. It is mine. All mine.

Two-Minute Girl

(In some schools, two minutes before classes start,
a Two-Minute Girl or Boy pokes his or her head round
the Staffroom door and warns the teachers to Get Ready)

I'm the Two-Minute Girl
I'm about the size of a briefcase
I have bunches done up with barbed wire
And Count Dracula pointy teeth

I'm the Two-Minute Girl
I'm as sweet as syrup pudding on the surface
But I'm as wicked as stinging nettles underneath

Two minutes early or two minutes late
I stick my head round the staffroom door
And sometimes I whisper like the ghost of a snake
(two minutes) and leave the teachers to snore

Yes I'm the Two-Minute Girl
I'm as cunning as cunning can be
With the driving brain of a diesel train
And the mischieviousness of a flea

Oh I'm the Two-Minute Girl
I love to spread the Two-Minute Blues
Especially when I bellow TWO MINUTES!
And a teacher pours the teapot all over his new suede shoes

Lost Love Poem

One day they'll manufacture eggs,
The formula for snowflakes will be clear
And love explained – that's not the day
I think about, the day I marked on my calendar.

Because they appreciate their legs,
Simple creatures will career
Through boundless grass. One day, the day
I think about, the day I marked on my calendar.

In the classroom the boy with ragged fingernails
Flicks a note to the girl whose hair solidifies
All the light there is. The note says:
Some day, when I'm grown up, some day –
It falls between the floorboards...

The Blackboard

Five foot by five foot
(The smalls have measured it).
Smooth black surface
(Wiped by a small after every class).
Five different colours of chalk
And a class of twenty-five smalls,
One big.

Does the big break up the chalk
Into twenty-five or twenty-six
And invite the smalls to make
A firework show of colours
Shapes and words
Starting on the blackboard
But soon overflowing
All over the room
   All over the school
      All over the town
         All over the country
            All over the world?

   No.

The big looks at the textbook
Which was written by a big
And published by a firm of bigs.
The textbook says
The names and dates of Nelson's battles.
So the big writes, in white,
Upon the black of the blackboard,
The names and dates of Nelson's battles.
The smalls copy into their books
The names and dates of Nelson's battles.

   Nelson was a big
Who died fighting for freedom or something.

Teachers Are Not Allowed To Take Their Clothes Off

This is a new rule
It was not thought necessary
But a new teacher came to school
There she was in the staffroom with nothing on
The School Secretary said to her
You were wearing clothes when we interviewed you
Yes said the new nude teacher
But I was so pleased to get a job
That I went home and took off my clothes
And my cats took one look at me
And started to sing and dance
So I burned all my clothes
And I feel much better.
This is the reason for the new rule.

School Dinners

Lumpy custard and liver – ugh!
I hate school dinners and I'll tell you why.
There's dog food with peas in, there's Secret Stew,
And a cheese and bacon thing we call Sick Pie.

Back In The Playground Blues

I dreamed I was back in the playground, I was about four feet high
Yes dreamed I was back in the playground, standing about four
    feet high
Well the playground was three miles long and the playground was
    five miles wide

It was broken black tarmac with a high wire fence all around
Broken black dusty tarmac with a high fence running all around
And it had a special name to it, they called it The Killing Ground

Got a mother and a father, they're one thousand years away
The rulers of The Killing Ground are coming out to play
Everybody thinking: "Who they going to play with today?"

    Well you get it for being Jewish
    And you get it for being black
    Get it for being chicken
    And you get it for fighting back
    You get it for being big and fat
    Get it for being small
    Oh those who get it get it and get it
    For any damn thing at all

Sometimes they take a beetle, tear off its six legs one by one
Beetle on its black back, rocking in the lunchtime sun
But a beetle can't beg for mercy, a beetle's not half the fun

I heard a deep voice talking, it had that iceberg sound
"It prepares them for Life" – but I have never found
Any place in my life worse than The Killing Ground.

How To Write Poems

Bite your lower lip,
Stick out your tongue.
That's the way
The poems get done.

Screw up your eyes,
Take a new look.
That's the way
Poems start to cook.

Elephantasia

an island of assorted animals
ruled over by a wise and
cheerful herd of tuskers

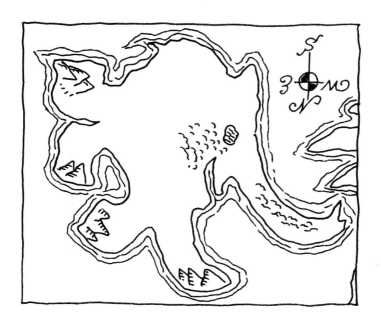

Nature Poem

Skylark, what prompts your silver song
To fountain up and down the sky?

Beetles roast
With fleas on toast
And earthworm pie.

Yorkshire Epitaph

he could run right fast

a ginger-golden hump of fur
but his retractable feet could move over the Yorkshire grass
so we called him after the best runner we could remember
    Zatopec

after a night of frost
found dead in his netted house
legs straight out
a dark stain round his mouth
a globe tear in the corner of one eye
he was buried in the flower bed
    Zatopec, our lone guinea pig

he could run right fast

Not A Very Cheerful Song, I'm Afraid

There was a gloomy lady,
With a gloomy duck and a gloomy drake,
And they all three wandered gloomily,
Beside a gloomy lake,
On a gloomy, gloomy, gloomy, gloomy, gloomy, gloomy day.

Now underneath that gloomy lake
The gloomy lady's gone.
But the gloomy duck and the gloomy drake
Swim on and on and on,
On a gloomy, gloomy, gloomy, gloomy, gloomy, gloomy day.

Rat It Up

C'mon everybody
Slap some grease on those paws
Get some yellow on your teeth
And, uh, sharpen up your claws

There's a whole lot of sausage
We're gonna swallow down
We're gonna jump out the sewers
And rock this town

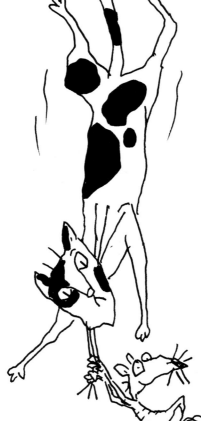

Cos we're ratting it up
Yes we're ratting it up
Well we're ratting it up
For a ratting good time tonight

Ain't got no compass
You don't need no map
Just follow your snout
Hey, watch out for that trap!

You can take out a poodle
You can beat up a cat
But if you can't lick a ferret
You ain't no kind of rat

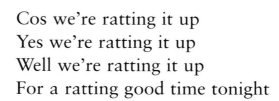

Cos we're ratting it up
Yes we're ratting it up
Well we're ratting it up
For a ratting good time tonight

Now you can sneak in the henhouse
Roll out the eggs
But if the farmer comes running
Bite his hairy legs

Check that cheese for poison
Before you eat
Or you'll wind up being served up
As ratburger meat

Cos we're ratting it up
Yes we're ratting it up
Well we're ratting it up
For a ratting good time tonight

This rat was born to rock
This rat was born to roll
I don't give a monkey's
Bout your pest control

So push off pussy-cat
Push off pup
We're the Rockin' Rodents
And we're ratting it up

Yeah we're ratting it up
Yeah we're ratting it up
Well we're ratting it up
For a ratting good time tonight!

Hog In A Wood

Big black hog in a wood
On a truffle hunt.
Head stuck deep in the earth –
Grunt, snort, grunt.

Oh a hog's in heaven when his tongue
Is wrapped around a truffle.
His tail uncurls and his hog heart
Performs a soft-shoe shuffle.

Big black hog in a wood
Chewing muddy truffles.
Great snout nosing them out –
Sniff, snuff, snuffles.

Understanding The Rain

(for a horse called Elgin)

Top right-hand corner
Of a South Devon field
The great white horse
Stands under the warm rain

Slow-motion grass
Growing greener and greener
The great white horse
Stands under the warm rain

Like a shining cathedral
Under the centuries
The great white horse
Stands under the warm rain

Like a waiting messenger
Like the people of England
Like the planet Earth
Like poetry
Like a great white horse
The great white horse
Stands under the warm rain

Never Forget The Birthday Of Anyone Who Has Antlers Bigger Than Your Body

No excuse
Is any use
To a deeply offended Moose

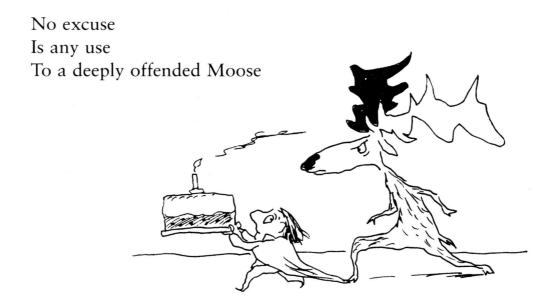

Cookery Advice

If stuck in a kitchen
With a hungry leopard
Ask him: Would you like me
Salted and peppered?

Revenge

The elephant knocked the ground with a stick,
He knocked it slow, he knocked it quick.
He knocked it till his trunk turned black –
Then the ground turned round and knocked him back.

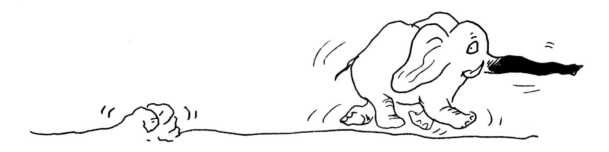

The Galactic Pachyderm

The elephant stands
      among the stars
He jumps off
      Neptune
bounces off
      Mars
to adventures on
      Venus
while his children
      play
in the diamond jungles
      of the
Milky Way

Tinkling The Ivories

There was an elephant
    called Art Tatum
He played a piano
    whose keys were human teeth

Non-Event

If an elephant could meet a whale
their understanding would be huge
and they would love one another for ever

Pride

The elephant
is not proud of being an elephant
So why are we ashamed?

Good Taste

The vilest furniture in this land
is an elephant's foot umbrella stand

Love Poem, Elephant Poem

Elephants are as amazing as love
but love is as amazing as elephants
Love is as amazing as elephants
but elephants are as amazing as love

You Aren't What You Eat

The elephant
who's seldom flustered
despises calming food
like custard
Devouring curry
in a hurry
washed down with
a mug of mustard

The Infant Elephant Speaks:

I got a rusk
stuck on my tusk

Turn Turn Turn

There is a time for considering elephants
There is no time for not considering elephants

Elephant Eternity

Elephants walking under juicy-leaf trees
Walking with their children under juicy-leaf trees
Elephants elephants walking like time

Elephants bathing in the foam-floody river
Fountaining their children in the mothery river
Elephants elephants bathing like happiness

    Strong and gentle elephants
    Standing on the earth
    Strong and gentle elephants
    Like peace

Time is walking under elephant trees
Happiness is bathing in the elephant river
Strong gentle peace is shining
All over the elephant earth

Spookalulu

where there are heroes on
the purple hills and monsters
lurking in the chilly caves

Third Time Unlucky

ghosts playing dice
with dice made of ice
they let you win once
they let you win twice

Official Notice

Persons with Dogs or Chimpanzees:
Try to distract their attention, please,
When promenading past the Giant Cheese.

Golo, The Gloomy Goalkeeper

Golo plays for the greatest soccer team in the Universe.
They are so mighty that their opponents never venture out
    of their own penalty area.
They are so all-conquering that Golo never touches the ball
    during a match, and very seldom sees it.
Every game seems to last a lifetime to Golo,
    the Gloomy Goalkeeper.

Golo scratches white paint off the goalposts' surface to reveal
    the silver shining underneath.
He kisses the silver of the goalpost.
It does not respond.

He counts the small stones in the penalty area.
There are three hundred and seventy eight, which is not
    his lucky number.
Golo pretends to have the hiccups, then says to himself,
    imitating his sister's voice:
Don't breathe, and just die basically.

He breaks eight small sticks in half.
Then he has sixteen very small sticks.
He plants geranium seeds along the goal-line.
He paints a picture of a banana and sells it to the referee
    at half-time.

Golo finds, among the bootmarks in the dust, the print of
    one stiletto heel.
He crawls around on all fours doing lion imitations.
He tries to read his future in the palm of his hand, but
    forgets to take his glove off.

He writes a great poem about butterflies but tears it up
    because he can't think of a rhyme for Wednesday.
He knits a sweater for the camel in the zoo.

Golo suddenly realises he can't remember if he is a man
    or a woman.
He takes a quick look, but still can't decide.

He makes up his mind that grass is his favourite colour.
He puts on boots, track-suit, gloves and hat all the same
    colour as grass.
He paints his face a gentle shade of green.

He lies down on the pitch and becomes invisible.
The grass tickles the back of his neck.
At last Golo is happy.
He has fallen in love with the grass.
And the grass has fallen in love with Golo,
    the Gloomy Goalkeeper.

Unlucky Steps

Thirteen steps
Leading me down
Down to that big blue door
Big blue door
With a grime-lined face
And a voice like a polar bear roar,
The sound of a mechanized blizzard
Which froze my trainers to the floor.

It sounded like a cloud of poison gas
Whispering evil to itself.
It sounded like a bunch of defrosting cobras
Slithering off their shelf.

I pushed down the handle
The handle stayed down
For three point five seconds at least
Then the handle sprang back
And the wild white sound
Of a beast that longed to be released
Suddenly stopped.

The silence swelled and swelled and swelled
As if it were about to burst.
My heart felt like a blue iced lolly
    On an ice rink
       In Alaska
          On December the 21st.

I backed up the steps
    13, 12, 11
Away from the cupboard of snows
I backed up the steps
    10, 9, 8, 7
I don't want to join the Eskimos
I backed up the steps
    6, 5, 4
My heart saying: Go man, go man!
I backed up the steps
Then I turned around –
That's when I got eaten by a Snowman.

The Set-Square, Square-Set Gunman

(for geometricians and Country and Western fans)

I come from Euclid County, where the savage Cosines ride
And under the Geomma Tree I tunes my old guitar.
My pappy was a Cube who took a Spiral fer his bride
So I wuz born to be rectangular.

Yup. Both my sides is parallel and I'm broader than I'm high,
But have no doubt about my shoot-it-out capacity,
Fer I've got more angles than Isosceles, plus a Pythagorean eye
And all the cowpokes call me Oblong Cassidy.

The Floating Flautist

I wish I lived in a house in the clouds:
I'd serenade wing-clapping seagull crowds.
My flute would purr and ripple and trill
And angels would perch on my window-sill.

Their Voices

One had a voice like an ancient wooden desk
Initials cut deep all over
And then inked in, black, blue and blue-black.

Two had a voice like a rubbish dump –
Old cabbages tumbling out of a sack.

Three had a voice like a fountain on a mountain
And a holiday stream bounding down the rocks.

Four had a voice like a willow-tree.

Five had a voice like a jack-in-the-box.

But what did they say? What decisions were made?
Dunno. I only listened to the music they played.

I Am Boj

*(to be shouted, in the voice of a terrible giant,
at children who wake early).*

I am Boj
I crackle like the Wig of a Judge

I am Boj
My eyes boil over with Hodge-Podge

I am Boj
Organised Sludge and a Thunder-Wedge

I am Boj
I am a Tower of solid Grudge

I am Boj
The molten Centre, the cutting Edge

I am Boj
From deepest Dudgeon I swing my Bludgeon

I am Boj

Giving Potatoes

Strong Man:
Mashed potatoes cannot hurt you, darling
Mashed potatoes mean no harm
I have brought you mashed potatoes
From my mashed potato farm.

Lady:
Take away your mashed potatoes
Leave them in the desert to dry
Take away your mashed potatoes –
You look like shepherd's pie.

Brash Man:
A packet of chips, a packet of chips,
Wrapped in the *Daily Mail*,
Golden and juicy and fried for a week
In the blubber of the Great White Whale.

Lady:
Take away your fried potatoes
Use them to clean your ears
You can eat your fried potatoes
With Birds-Eye frozen tears.

Old Man:
I have borne this baked potato
O'er the Generation Gap,
Pray accept this baked potato
Let me lay it in your heated lap.

Lady:
Take away your baked potato
In your fusty musty van
Take away your baked potato
You potato-skinned old man.

Frenchman:
She rejected all potatoes
For a thousand night and days
Till a Frenchman wooed and won her
With pommes de terre Lyonnaises.

Lady:
Oh my corrugated lover
So creamy and so brown
Let us fly across to Lyons
And lay our tubers down.

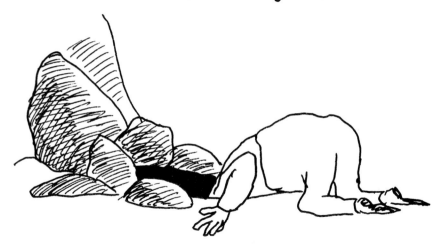

What's That Down There?

What's that down there?
What's that moving?
What's that moving down in the dark
    of this chilly black maze of a cave?

Is it Sarallo –
The scarlet snake with the seven
Silver heads
And fangs that snap like a murder trap?

What's that down there?
What's that moving?
What's that moving down in the dark
    of this chilly black maze of a cave?

Is it Farranaway –
That back-cracking brute
With a hundred horns
And hoofs that hit like horrible hammers?

What's that down there?
What's that moving?
What's that moving down in the dark
    of this chilly black maze of a cave?

Is it Thilissa –
That slippery wisp of
A whispering ghost of a
Girl who died
In the moistness of mist
Which lies like a shroud on
The underground lake
down in the dark in this chilly black maze of a cave?

The Gondoliers of Greenland

The Gondoliers of Greenland
Are the Grumpiest folk in the North
Their canals melt on August the Second
And freeze up on August the Fourth.
In those two laborious glorious days
All their incomes must be made
And the rest of the year they wait listlessly
To ply their ridiculous trade.

Balloon Lagoon

in whose blue waters you
may see reflected views
of the strange Planet Earth

Song In Space

When man first flew beyond the sky
He looked back into the world's blue eye.
Man said: What makes your eye so blue?
Earth said: The tears in the ocean do.
Why are the seas so full of tears?
Because I've wept so many thousand years.
Why do you weep as you dance through space?
Because I am the Mother of the Human Race.

Keep Your Airplanes Away From Our Islands

the islands of Toronto
sleep upon the waters

small grass and friendly trees
are talking to the giant sky

a garter snake whispers across the path
the tyres of a bicycle whisper back

you can hear my brother singing to his boots
a squeaky song about the olden days
as the swing creaks him up to the sun

my mother plays the flute and her music makes
a fountain of birds fountain over the waters

you can hear so much on these lovely islands
which rose from the lake in an age of silence

you can hear the breathing of your best friend
you can hear the blood swimming around your veins

you can hear a slow and barefoot tread
which I believe is the sound of peace walking

peace upon the islands
peace upon the waters

as the islands of Toronto
sleep on the holy waters

99

Thankful For A Rainfall

A Pyrrenhean Mountain Dog
Sprawls on a sofa

An early, furry mist
Lies all along the river

Two trees lean against a third
Still discussing last year's storm

Last night's rain has travelled up to London
Blobs from the rim of my hut remember him

Sunshine tickles
The thankful thistles

Butterflies stumble around the breeze
Cats tip-toe among brand-new puddles

Blessings roll down the earth's dusty red throat
And the sky has come straight from the washing machine

The Mighty Man
On The Mower

In my soft and silver helmet
I ride across the plain
For I am proud and supple
And happy as the moon.

My chariot was made of steel
For Saladin the Saracen.
It is drawn by a dragon
Whose roaring mouth spouts flames of green...

The Big Fall

I'm a leaf that came to grief, chief,
Fell off that good old tree,
Flittered and fluttered down to the ground –
Why did it have to be meedle-e-dee
Why did it have to be me?

I was happy as a humbug in my good old tree
But now I'm all flopsome and lost.
I get all soggy in the thumpering rain
And I crinkle like a cornflake in the frost.
O yes, I crunkle like a flornflake in the frost.

So carry me away to the compost heap
With ten thousand other loose leaves like me.
I'll be happy as a hamster in the compost heap
Dreaming of my good old treedle-e-dee
Dreaming of my good old tree.

Winter Listening

Humble, crumbly song of the snails.
Pinecones rattling in a stormy tree.
The frosty voices of December stars.
Dragon-roaring of a scarlet factory.

Honking slapstick of seals at play.
The creak and slish of snow off a roof.
Crackle-whisper of Christmas paper.
The silver step of a unicorn's hoof.

Winter Bully

Somebody beat up November the Tenth –
(Maybe December the First) –
It wore a sky like a black eye
And was crying fit to burst.

Round and Round

The handle swings the mallet
The mallet drives the wedge
The wedge cracks the tree trunk
With its cutting edge
The chainsaw comes roaring in to fell it
Then a carpenter takes a slice of the tree
And carves out the handle for a mallet

A Speck Speaks

About ten million years ago
I was a speck of rock in a vast black rock.
My address was:
      Vast Black Rock,
      Near Italy,
      Twelve Metres Under
The Mediterranean Sea.

The other specks and I
Formed an impressive edifice –
Bulbously curving at the base
With rounded caves
And fun tunnels for the fish,
Romantically jagged at the top.

Life, for us specks, was uneventful –
One for all, welded together
In the cool, salty wet.
What more could specks
Expect?

Each year a few of us were lost,
Scrubbed from the edges of the rock
By the washerwoman waters
Which smoothed our base, whittled our cornices
And sharpened our pinnacles.
As the rock slowly shed skin-thin layers
It was my turn to be exposed
Among the packed grit of its surface,
(Near the tip of the fifty-ninth spire
From the end of the eastern outcrop).

One day, it was a Wednesday I remember,
A scampi flicked me off my perch
Near the vast black rock's peak
And I was scurried down
Long corridors of currents
Until a wave caught me in its mouth
And spat me out on –
What?

A drying stretch
Of yellow, white, black, red and transparent specks,
Billions of particles,
Loosely organized in bumps and dips;
Quite unlike the tight hard group
Which I belonged to in the good old rock.
Heat banged down on us all day long.
Us? I turned to the speck next to me,
 A lumpish red fellow who'd been washed off a brick.

"I'm new here," I confessed,
"What are we supposed to be?"
He bellowed back –
(But the bellow of a speck
Is less than the whispering of ants) –
"We're grains now, grains of sand,
And this society is called Beach."

"Beach?" I said. "What are we grains supposed to do?"
"Just stray around, lie loose,
Go with the wind, go with the sea
And sink down when you're trodden on."
"Don't know if I can manage that.
Used to belong to Vast Black Rock
And we all stuck together."

"Give Beach a try," said the red grain.
Well, there was no alternative.

Many eras later
I was just beginning to feel
Part of Beach, that slow-drifting,
Slow-shifting, casual community,
When I was shovelled up
With a ton of fellow grains,
Hoisted into a lorry, shaken down a road,
Washed, sifted and poured in a machine
Hotter than the sunshine.

When they poured me out, life had changed again.
My mates and I swam in a molten river
Down into a mould.
White-hot we were, then red, then
Suddenly cold
And we found ourselves merged
Into a tall, circular tower,
Wide at the bottom, narrow at the top
What's more, we'd all turned green as sea-weed.
Tranparent green.
We had become – a wine bottle.

In a few flashes of time
We'd been filled with wine,
Stoppered, labelled, bumped to a shop,
Stood in a window, sold, refrigerated,
Drained by English tourists,
Transmogrified into a lampstand,
Smashed by a four-year-old called Tarquin,
Swept up, chucked in the garbage, hauled away,
Dumped and bulldozed into the sea.

Now the underwater years sandpaper away
My shield-shaped fragment of bottle.
So one day I shall be a single grain again,
A single grain of green, transparent glass.

When that day comes
I will transmit a sub-aquatic call
To all green specks of glass
Proposing that we form
A Vast Green Rock of Glass,
Near Italy,
Twelve Metres Under
The Mediterranean Sea.

Should be pretty spectacular
In about ten million years.

All being well.

A Child Is Singing

A child is singing
And nobody listening
But the child who is singing:

Bulldozers grab the earth and shower it.
    The house is on fire.
Gardeners wet the earth and flower it.
    The house is on fire.
    The houses are on fire.
Fetch the fire engine, the fire engine's on fire.
    We will have to hide in a hole.
    We will burn slow, like coal.
    All the people are on fire.

And a child is singing
And nobody listening
But the child who is singing.

A Valentine Poem

For Cathy Pompe's Kids
At St Paul's Primary School, Cambridge
(who were about 6 – 7 years old)

The night is a dark blue balloon
The day is a golden balloon
The moon longs to cuddle the sun
The sun longs to cuddle the moon

Goodbye